The Airship

"Dedicated to Wendy"
This story tells the value of having
a dream to follow.

Story by:
Ken Forsse

Illustrated by:
David High
Russell Hicks
Valerie Edwards
Rennie Rau

WORLDS OF WONDER™

Grubby™ Newton Gimmick™ Princess Aruzia™ Leota™ Wooly What's-It™

Prince Arin™ Fobs™

Grubby's been a good friend
of mine for a long time.

Your friend, your friend is what I'd like to be.

The treasure was supposed to be hidden in the far off land of Grundo.

Oh, hello there, my name
is Newton Gimmick.

I call it an airship. Hmm, it looks like a boat.

The hot air will rise and cause the ship to lift off the ground.

The ship lifted off the
ground and Gimmick
was delighted with his
invention.

The airship had turned
upside down and crashed.

We could make the airship go up and down okay, but we couldn't steer it very well.

She was a real woodsprite, no bigger than a bird...and very pretty.

Leota gave us some ideas about steering the airship.

Come and discover the
world with me.